UNDERSTANDING THE
BLACK LIVES MATTER MOVEMENT

RAGE AND PROTESTS ACROSS THE COUNTRY

by Clara MacCarald

BrightPoint Press

San Diego, CA

BrightP◇int Press

For more information, contact:
BrightPoint Press
PO Box 27779
San Diego, CA 92198
www.BrightPointPress.com

LIBRARY OF CONGRESS CATALOGING-IN-PUBLICATION DATA

Names: MacCarald, Clara, 1979- author.
Title: Rage and protests across the country / by Clara MacCarald.
Description: San Diego, CA : BrightPoint Press, [2021] | Series: Understanding the Black
   Lives Matter movement | Includes bibliographical references and index. | Audience:
   Grades 7-9 | Summary: "After police in Minnesota killed George Floyd, an unarmed Black
   man, in May 2020, protests spread across the country and even throughout the world.
   While most protesters were peaceful, violence also broke out at some protests. Rage and
   Protests Across the Country examines the Black Lives Matter protests of 2020 and how
   they affected the movement"-- Provided by publisher.
Identifiers: LCCN 2020047440 (print) | LCCN 2020047441 (eBook) | ISBN 9781678200725
   (hardcover) | ISBN 9781678200732 (eBook)
Subjects: LCSH: Black lives matter movement--Juvenile literature. | Protest movements-
   -United States--History--21st century--Juvenile literature. | African Americans--Social
   conditions--21st century--Juvenile literature. | Racism--United States--21st century--
   Juvenile literature. | Racial profiling in law enforcement--United States--Juvenile literature. |
   Police shootings--Juvenile literature. | United States--Race relations--Juvenile literature.
Classification: LCC E185.86 .M3117 2021 (print) | LCC E185.86 (eBook) | DDC 303.48/4--
   dc23
LC record available at https://lccn.loc.gov/2020047440
LC eBook record available at https://lccn.loc.gov/2020047441

CONTENTS

AT A GLANCE

- The Black Lives Matter movement started in 2013. People in the movement aimed to fight racism and police brutality while uplifting Black people.

- On March 25, 2020, George Floyd died. A police officer had knelt on his neck for several minutes. Videos of the event spread rapidly on social media.

- Millions of people protested after Floyd's death. People of all races and ages expressed rage at what had happened. Events happened in communities of many sizes across America and around the world.

- Some protests led to disorder. Some people looted stores and started fires. But more than 90 percent of the Black Lives Matter protests were peaceful.

- Some police forces wore heavy gear and tried to control crowds with tear gas and rubber bullets. A few officers marched or knelt with protesters to show support.

- Protesters wanted justice for Black people killed by police. Some wanted police reform and other political changes.

- Some state and local governments made changes in their police departments after Floyd's death, such as banning choke holds.

- In the summer after Floyd's death, Black Lives Matter protests continued in many cities. The protest movement showed no sign of stopping by the fall of 2020.

POLICE AND PROTESTERS

On June 1, 2020, people filled Lafayette Park in Washington, DC. Black Lives Matter protests like this one had been going on for days. The crowd was protesting **police brutality**. People of all races gathered. Some held signs. Many wore face masks to guard against disease. At the time, the coronavirus **pandemic** was

Peaceful protesters filled Lafayette Park as the Black Lives Matter movement grew in the summer of 2020.

affecting the world. Everyone at this event was protesting peacefully.

The night before, though, protests had turned violent. A fire had broken out in nearby Saint John's Church. Despite the fire, leaders of Saint John's Church had come for that day's protest. Church leaders offered snacks and water to the crowd.

Lines of police stood at the edge of the protest. Behind them officers sat on horseback. The police officers wore heavy gear. They held clear shields and wore helmets. The officers were there because of the earlier violence. Today, no one was causing trouble.

But the mood suddenly changed. Police rushed toward protesters. Officers slammed their shields into people. Chemical smoke

Trump walked with other officials and security forces across the park after police cleared out protesters.

filled the park, choking protesters. The park

cleared as people ran to safety.

In the calm left behind, President Donald

Trump appeared. He walked between the

lines of police all the way to Saint John's

Church. In front of the church, Trump held up a Bible. He said, "We have the greatest country in the world. Keep it nice and safe."[1]

A GLOBAL MOVEMENT

The following day, crowds returned to continue the Black Lives Matter protest. Black Lives Matter (BLM) is a global movement. Its goal is to stop racism and violence against Black people.

BLM began in 2013. The movement grew in the following years. An incident in 2020 made it bigger than ever before. On May 25, a Black man named George Floyd died in Minneapolis, Minnesota. A police officer had

BLM protests drew millions of Americans in the summer of 2020.

knelt on his neck for around eight minutes.

A wave of pain and anger spread rapidly.

Millions took to the streets to call for justice.

CHAPTER ONE

WHY HAVE BLM PROTESTS HAPPENED?

The BLM movement began as a response to tragedy. In February 2012, Black teenager Trayvon Martin walked through a Florida neighborhood. He was unarmed. George Zimmerman noticed him. Zimmerman belonged to the neighborhood watch. Zimmerman

The killing of Trayvon Martin helped lead to the creation of the BLM movement.

called the police. He said Trayvon looked

suspicious. He noted Trayvon was wearing

a hoodie. The dispatcher told him not to

approach Trayvon. Zimmerman did anyway.

During a fight, Zimmerman shot and killed

Trayvon. He claimed he had shot the teen in self-defense.

When the story became public, people were upset that the police had not arrested Zimmerman. Protests broke out across the country. Protesters held signs calling for justice for Trayvon. They also wanted justice for other Black people who had been killed, many by police officers. People in the crowds often wore hooded sweatshirts like the one Trayvon had been wearing.

In 2013, a court ruled that Zimmerman was not guilty of murder. Three Black women, Alicia Garza, Patrisse Cullors, and

Opal Tometi was one of the women who started BLM.

Opal Tometi, decided they'd had enough.

They started a movement called Black Lives

Matter. A social media **hashtag** helped

spread the word. But over time, more

deaths happened. **Activists** connected to

BLM moved their organizing to the streets.

MORE DEATHS, MORE PROTESTS

In the summer of 2014, the deaths of two unarmed Black men sparked waves of protests. In New York City, police officer Daniel Pantaleo put Eric Garner in a choke hold. The police suspected Garner was selling cigarettes without a license. Garner kept repeating, "I can't breathe," until he died. Someone nearby filmed Garner's death. The video spread around the world. Pantaleo denied that he had used a choke hold. A police department official did not accept this explanation, and Pantaleo was eventually fired in 2019.

"I can't breathe" became a common protest slogan following Garner's death.

In Ferguson, Missouri, an officer shot and killed eighteen-year-old Michael Brown Jr. Police officer Darren Wilson stopped Brown and a friend in the street. Wilson and Brown's friend told different stories about what happened next. Wilson said Brown was charging toward him ready to attack. Brown's friend said that Wilson had threatened them. But no one had filmed the events leading to Brown's death.

After the shooting, Brown's body lay in the street for more than four hours. People in the community and around the country were outraged. That night, people set up a memorial where Brown had died. Officers were on the scene with weapons and dogs.

The next day, protesters gathered in Ferguson. They held candles to mourn Brown. Officers nearby were in armored cars, wore body armor, and carried assault weapons. A few protesters may have reacted to this show of force with violence.

People set up memorials near where Brown had been killed.

Some people damaged property or stole things. The police shot tear gas and rubber bullets to try to control the crowds.

A police shooting in Cleveland, Ohio, ignited additional protests in November 2014. A twelve-year-old Black boy, Tamir Rice, was playing in a park. He had a toy pellet gun. Someone called the police, saying a person was pointing a gun at people in the park. The caller said the person was probably a kid and the gun was likely fake. But this information was not passed to the officers. They drove up close to Tamir, and Officer Timothy Loehmann shot him within two seconds of arriving.

Groups of protesters marched in Cleveland in the coming weeks. Some blocked streets and the entrances to stores. They called for justice for Tamir.

JURIES AND INVESTIGATIONS

In November 2014, a **grand jury** considered the case in Ferguson. It would

The names of Tamir Rice and others killed by police became rallying cries for protesters.

soon decide whether to charge the officer

who killed Brown. Brown's parents asked

protesters to be peaceful. Brown's father

said, "I do not want my son's death to be in

vain. I want it to lead to incredible change,

positive change, change that makes the St. Louis region better for everyone."[2]

On November 24, the jury announced its decision. It would not charge the officer. President Barack Obama knew the result would anger many people. He gave a speech. He asked people to respect the law. He pointed out that the problems identified by protesters were real. But he said communities needed peaceful solutions. He called for communities and police to work together.

But people were furious with the police. Protests spread around the country. Many protesters chanted or displayed Garner's words: "I can't breathe." Others held their hands up, like some people thought Brown had done.

About a week after the Ferguson grand jury decision, officials in New York City made an announcement. The officer who had killed Garner would also not be

PROTEST SLOGANS

A slogan is a short saying used by a group or movement. Many slogans showed up at Black Lives Matter protests along with "I can't breathe." "Hands up, don't shoot" came from the belief that Brown held his hands in the air before his death. "No justice, no peace" was used in riots after police beat a Black man named Rodney King in 1991.

In the years to come, people would continue to demand justice for Garner.

charged. Thousands of protesters gathered

in the city. Some pretended to die in the

street. They wanted to call attention to the

deaths related to police violence. Other

protesters carried coffins. Police arrested

some protesters who would not move.

The anger in Ferguson led to

investigations. The federal government

looked into the police and courts of Ferguson. The government found racial bias in the local justice system. Police officers were more likely to arrest Black people than white people. Officers were more likely to use force on Black people. After Brown's death, several members of the Ferguson police force stepped down or were fired. But people felt this did not represent justice. They continued to protest.

A year later, in December 2015, a grand jury made its decision in the Tamir Rice case. As with the Brown and Garner cases, the officer would not be charged.

Protesters demonstrated outside Cleveland's Cuyahoga County Justice Center in December 2015.

Officials said the officers were justified to feel in danger due to the realistic toy gun. They blamed human error and miscommunication. But they did not believe the shooting was a crime. Protesters took to the streets of Cleveland, marching and blocking streets in frigid weather. People in several other cities around the country protested in support.

TAKING A KNEE

Protests spread to other parts of public life. As the BLM movement gained ground, sports figures joined in. Some players wore T-shirts bearing the words "I can't breathe." Some players wore the names of those who were killed.

Football star Colin Kaepernick became famous for his protests. At the beginning of each game, football teams usually stand for the national **anthem**. In 2016, Kaepernick began to sit instead. He was protesting

Colin Kaepernick's protests on the football field raised awareness of BLM.

police brutality. Later, he began to kneel. He thought kneeling still showed respect for the country and the anthem. People across the United States had differing opinions about Kaepernick. Some supported his actions. Others were angry at him. His team did not re-sign him the next season, and no other teams picked him up. Some fans felt he was being punished for his protest.

THE DEATH OF GEORGE FLOYD

In early 2020, the world faced a pandemic. A disease called COVID-19 was sickening and killing people around the globe. The disease easily spread from person to person. One way to stop it was to keep people from getting close to each other. In March 2020, schools and many businesses closed, and local governments asked people to stay home.

George Floyd lived in a suburb of Minneapolis, Minnesota. He was one of millions of people to lose their jobs due to COVID-19. On May 25, he went to a store. A worker accused him of using a fake bill. The police came and arrested Floyd. After a struggle, Floyd lay face down with his hands in handcuffs.

Officer Derek Chauvin knelt on Floyd's neck for around eight minutes. Floyd begged the officer to stop. He said he couldn't breathe. He cried out for his mother. Eventually, Floyd stopped moving. Another officer on the scene searched for a pulse and couldn't find one. An ambulance took Floyd to a nearby hospital.

He was pronounced dead there. The

police had body cameras recording the

events. Witnesses took videos as well.

These images would soon spark a renewed

protest movement across the country.

BODY CAMERAS

Body cameras are recording devices worn by police. Brown's family campaigned for police across the United States to wear the devices. With no recording of Brown's death, no one will know what actually happened. Body cameras have become more widespread since 2014. Video evidence can protect both police and the public. The presence of cameras may even cause police and suspects to behave better. Researchers continue to study how effective cameras are.

CHAPTER TWO

WHAT HAPPENED AFTER GEORGE FLOYD DIED?

The George Floyd video spread rapidly through social media. Viewers saw police officers disregard Floyd's pleas. The day after Floyd's death, protesters flooded Minneapolis streets. The local police chief fired the officers who were involved. But protesters wanted the officers arrested.

Early June 2020 saw huge protests and marches in Minneapolis.

In the following days, a large group surrounded a police station. Other protesters damaged police cars. The police responded as they had during previous unrest. Officers set off tear gas. They fired rubber bullets into the crowd. Many peaceful protesters were hit by these weapons. Other people set fires and looted stores. They burned down a Minneapolis police station.

PROTESTS SPREAD LIKE WILDFIRE

Within days, protests popped up in major cities around the United States. Some protests shut down roads. In Los Angeles, California, activists formed a human chain across a freeway. In Washington, DC, people protested near the White House. Protests continued in Minneapolis and neighboring Saint Paul.

Protesters linked arms to block the Hollywood Freeway in California.

Part of the reason the protests grew was that people could see what happened for themselves. The videos clearly showed what had occurred. Officers had tried to arrest Floyd. He refused to get in the police car, but he didn't attack anyone. Chauvin pinned him down with a knee on his neck for around eight minutes. That included two minutes after Floyd had stopped moving.

COVID-19 may have increased the size of the protests too. Many people had lost their jobs or were working from home. Members of the public had more time at home to watch and read about Floyd's death. They had more time to protest.

The public learned about other killings too. People in Kentucky protested about Breonna Taylor. Police had shot Taylor, a Black woman, in her apartment. In Georgia, protesters honored Ahmaud Arbery. Arbery had been killed earlier in the year while going for a jog. A group of three white men saw him. They were suspicious of what he was doing. They chased him with a truck.

BREONNA TAYLOR

Breonna Taylor was a Black woman living in Louisville, Kentucky. She worked in health care. In the early morning of March 13, 2020, police officers broke into Taylor's apartment. They were investigating a drug dealer Taylor used to date. They thought the dealer might have had drugs delivered to the apartment. But Taylor had done nothing wrong. The police were not wearing uniforms. Taylor's current boyfriend said he thought they were under attack, so he shot at the police. Officers returned fire. Several bullets hit Taylor, killing her.

One of the men shot him. Arbery's story came to wider attention in the summer.

BLM protests spread around the world. People in other countries gathered and marched. They showed support for Americans calling for justice. Activists also

AHMAUD ARBERY'S KILLERS

Ahmaud Arbery died on February 23, 2020. Police waited more than two months to arrest his killers. One of the men who chased him claimed he suspected Arbery had stolen things in the neighborhood. A local official said he believed the men were making a legal citizen's arrest. A citizen's arrest is when an individual stops someone who has committed a crime. The men lied about the shooting later. But a video showed what really happened. The three men were eventually charged with murder.

protested racism and police brutality in their own countries. In France, for example, people honored the memory of several Black French men killed by police.

WHAT WERE PROTESTS LIKE?

Protesters brought signs. They marched together. They chanted together. People created a memorial to Floyd at the site where he died. A carpet of flowers lay under a mural of Floyd. The names of other Black people who had been killed were included in the painting. A sculpture of a wooden fist representing the BLM movement was put up in the middle of the intersection.

Some peaceful protesters in Florida lay on the ground as Floyd had done.

Many activists called attention to the

length of time the officer knelt on Floyd.

The news had reported that the officer

knelt on Floyd's neck for eight minutes and

forty-six seconds. Protesters knelt in silence

for this amount of time. Protesters also staged die-ins. They lay as if dead for the same amount of time.

The vast majority of protests were peaceful. But some were not. At some protests, people set fires and smashed windows. Some people looted stores and vehicles. Angry rioters threw objects at police officers and hurt some of them. Police officers took action to try to stop the destruction. Sometimes the officers used weapons on people who weren't being violent. The disorder often became greater as night fell. To try to bring the events under control, many cities ordered **curfews**.

Authorities hoped to clear the streets before it was dark. Some cops expressed support for the protesters. They knelt or marched alongside protesters.

Some of the people who showed up at protests opposed the BLM movement. For example, sometimes white supremacists came. White supremacists believe white people are better than all other races. Police in Minneapolis identified a white supremacist who was breaking windows and encouraging destruction. White supremacists in other areas also tried to

People in Los Angeles wrecked a police car during a riot.

start violence. They may have hoped the

public would blame Black protesters.

Some white people who opposed the

protests attacked protesters in the streets.

Dozens of drivers hit people. Some did it by accident. Others did it on purpose.

White supremacists have clashed with antifa, a loosely organized movement which supports Black Lives Matter but believes in violence. There have also been shootings. A group of Trump supporters drove their cars near a protest in Portland. A protester shot and killed one of these men. Days later, police found the shooter. They shot and killed him, saying he had drawn a gun.

In Seattle, Washington, activists took over a section of the city. The local police withdrew from the area in early June to calm the situation. The activists declared

the area the Capitol Hill Organized Protest

(CHOP). Following violence and shootings,

the police cleared the area on July 1.

WHAT IS ANTIFA?

Antifa is short for anti-fascist. The term generally refers to a loose movement rather than one group. Some people in the movement call themselves or their groups antifa. Others simply share the belief that **fascism** and white supremacy should be fought with violence. Only a few thousand people in the United States support antifa. Antifa supporters have caused a small part of the violence related to BLM protests.

Protesters in Seattle gathered in a space they called the Capitol Hill Organized Protest (CHOP) in June.

PROTESTS AND COVID-19

COVID-19 spreads through the air. It hops

easily between people who are close

together. Some people worried that the

BLM protests would lead to waves of COVID-19 cases. Scientists began looking at the issue. They found no evidence of an increase in COVID-19 related to the protests.

People at BLM protests often took steps to stay safe. Being outdoors is better than being inside. Open space and fresh air help make it harder for the virus to spread. People often wore face masks too. This helps stop the virus from leaving a person's mouth or nose and spreading to others. Protesters sometimes gave out masks to those who did not have them.

CHAPTER THREE

WHAT WERE THE RESPONSES TO THE PROTESTS?

Most of the public experienced the protests in some way. As many as 21 million adults had protested by the middle of June 2020. People of all races participated. At home, viewers watched protest scenes on social media and in the news. Overhead videos showed the

All around the world, journalists and protesters recorded the events of the protests.

masses of people present. Some journalists

came through with cameras. They stopped

to chat with protesters.

About 93 percent of BLM protests were peaceful. However, researcher Roudabeh Kishi said, "There have been some violent demonstrations, and those tend to get a lot of media coverage."[3] Some news shows played lots of videos of rioting and looting.

Because of this, some viewers connected BLM protests to violence. Some people thought that activists wanted to create disorder. Still, 67 percent of American adults supported the movement in June 2020. Support dipped over the summer. But 55 percent still supported BLM by September.

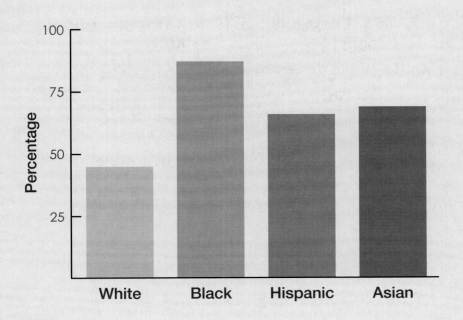

SUPPORT FOR BLM IN SEPTEMBER 2020

Deja Thomas and Juliana Menasce Horowitz,
"Support for Black Lives Matter Has Decreased Since
June but Remains Strong Among Black Americans,"
Pew Research Center, *September 16, 2020.*
www.pewresearch.org.

REACTING TO PROTESTS

President Trump frequently spoke about the

protests. He called them violent. He said

officials should take more aggressive action. He accused local leaders of being too weak to stop the violence.

In mid-2020, other people protested about restrictions due to the COVID-19 pandemic. Some people openly carried guns at these protests. Both these and BLM protests were mostly peaceful.

However, researchers noted that authorities used more violence during BLM protests. Officers were more likely to use tear gas, pepper spray, and rubber bullets. Law enforcement sometimes attacked journalists as well. Under US law, journalists can report freely on events. Some police

said they were unable to tell journalists

from rioters.

CLASHES IN PORTLAND

In general, violence from authorities did not

calm riots. One example was in Portland,

TEAR GAS AND PEPPER SPRAY

To control crowds, officers may use tear gas or pepper spray. Tear gas can mean one of several chemicals. The chemicals hang around in the air. Pepper spray contains a chemical which comes from peppers. The chemicals in both tear gas and pepper spray make it hard to see or breathe. People usually feel better after getting fresh air or flushing the chemicals out of their eyes. But large doses can cause blindness or even death.

Oregon. Riots happened regularly there after Floyd's death. Trump warned that the city had become lawless. Agents from the Department of Homeland Security arrived in early July.

Their presence angered many protesters. The Portland protests grew bigger. Thousands surrounded a federal courthouse every night. The federal agents began arresting people from the streets without identifying themselves.

Many shared videos of these arrests. People across the country condemned the behavior of the federal authorities.

The protests in Portland were passionate and long-lasting.

The mayors of several cities spoke up as well. They criticized the agents for not identifying themselves.

Not all activists were happy about the attention aimed at the courthouse clashes. Some felt it overshadowed the message of the protests.

Weeks after the federal agents arrived, Governor Kate Brown of Oregon made an agreement with the Trump administration. The agents would leave. Brown said, "The federal officers here in the city brought violence and they brought strife to our community. That needed to end."[4] For his part, Trump said the agents kept protesters from destroying Portland.

PROTESTS IN SPORTS

COVID-19 affected nearly every part of life, including sports. Sports leagues suspended their seasons. Sports restarted slowly. Games looked different from before. Teams played before empty stands.

SPORTS LEAGUES

It was not just individuals backing the protests. Sports leagues supported BLM as well. The National Football League added messages such as "End Racism" to its fields. The National Basketball Association displayed "Black Lives Matter" on its courts.

The NBA and its players came out strongly in support of the BLM movement.

Amid the uncertainty in the sports

world came the video of Floyd's death.

The response was very different from

athletes' protests years earlier. Now, it

wasn't just a few players. Many coaches

and players spoke out against racism and

police brutality. Players took a knee or raised a fist during the national anthem. Many athletes wore BLM shirts or the names of the people who had been killed.

In August 2020, police shot a Black man named Jacob Blake in Kenosha, Wisconsin. The Milwaukee Bucks basketball team protested by pulling out of an upcoming game. Basketball, baseball, and soccer leagues all delayed games as well. Players from the Women's National Basketball Association wore shirts with bullet holes painted on the back. Blake had been facing away from the police when he was shot.

WHAT HAVE BLM PROTESTS ACCOMPLISHED?

The people attending BLM protests didn't belong to a single group. Everyone had different ideas of how to move forward. Some wanted to change their local communities and police. Others wanted to reshape police departments across the country.

The events of 2020 brought many new people into the movement.

No matter their goals, police brutality brought them all together. YahNé Ndgo of Black Lives Matter Philadelphia said, "The ultimate demand is the end to violence, to end the war against black life."[5]

Protesters have not received everything they demanded. But some places are making important changes. In other cases, attempts to change policing have faltered. As long as racism and injustice keep harming Black people, the BLM protests are likely to continue.

JUSTICE FOR FLOYD AND TAYLOR

The four officers involved in the Floyd case were arrested. Chauvin faced murder charges. The others faced lesser charges.

Protesters wanted the men who shot Taylor to also go on trial. People protested in Louisville for months. They demanded

Chauvin was arrested on May 29 and charged with murder.

justice. However, a grand jury decided there was not enough evidence to charge the officers with murder. The court charged only one of the men. He faced charges for endangering neighbors with his careless shooting.

Protesters continued to demand justice for Breonna Taylor throughout 2020.

Officials announced the decision on September 23. Angry protesters poured into downtown Louisville. Kentucky lawmaker Charles Booker told them, "Keep demanding change . . . but don't be quiet, don't slow down, and most importantly, lean in with love."[6] Some protesters turned violent. Two police officers were injured by gunshots during the protests.

The protesters didn't get the justice they wanted in court. However, the city of Louisville promised Taylor's family it would reform the local police. It also agreed to a $12 million settlement with the family.

POLICE REFORM

Louisville outlined many new measures. Police officers would be encouraged to live in the communities they served. Police searches would need to be approved by higher-ranking commanders. Louisville banned no-knock warrants like the one that

police used when Taylor was killed.

Activists had many ideas for changing

policies after Floyd's death. One popular

idea was defunding the police. Some

reforms happened right away. Several

WHAT IS DEFUNDING THE POLICE?

To many people, defunding the police sounds like shutting down police entirely. Some activists do seek that. But for most people, defunding the police is different. It means shifting some police funding to other uses. Activists want that money to go toward services such as schools, hospitals, and social programs. They feel this could prevent crimes from happening in the first place.

state and local governments banned
choke holds.

In Minneapolis, the city council vowed to
disband the local police. The move would
take a long time and could be stopped
by voters. Some in the city supported
this, while others opposed the idea. It did
not end up happening in 2020. But the
city did shift funds away from the police.
The council gave $1.1 million to the health
department. The idea was that people
from the health department could address
conflicts before they turned violent.

Representative Karen Bass of California introduced the George Floyd Justice in Policing Act.

The US Congress tried to address police brutality in June. One bill was sponsored by Democrats. The law, named for Floyd, would have reformed police departments across the country. It would have made it easier to charge officers. It would have expanded the bans on choke holds.

Another bill was sponsored by Republicans.

It would have increased body camera

usage. It also included more training on

resolving situations peacefully. Neither law

passed in 2020.

SYMBOLS OF RACISM

Many southern states belonged to the

Confederacy during the American Civil

War (1861–1865). The Confederacy had

tried to break away from the United States.

It wanted to continue the practice of

slavery. Slavery ended in America after the

Confederacy was defeated.

In 2016, researchers noted more than 1,500 tributes to the Confederacy in the United States. More than 700 were monuments and statues. Many were put up long after the Civil War. They were meant to intimidate Black people who were fighting for their rights. Lawyer Richard Cohen, an expert on hate groups, said, "In many cases, preserving history was not the true goal of these displays."[7]

Activists have called for symbols of the Confederacy to be taken down. In the past, such activists have encountered a lot of resistance. But after Floyd's

In June, protesters demonstrated at a statue of Confederate general Robert E. Lee in Richmond, Virginia.

death, more than 130 such displays

came down. Protesters illegally knocked

down or damaged some of the statues.

Local governments moved or changed

others. The sports world was affected too.

The racing organization NASCAR banned

Confederate flags at its races.

THE COMMITMENT MARCH

On August 28, 1963, Dr. Martin Luther King Jr. gave his famous "I Have a Dream" speech in Washington, DC. In front of about 250,000 people, King mentioned many hardships Black people faced, including police brutality. The struggle continued 57 years later. On August 28, 2020, crowds gathered again for an event called the Commitment March: Get Your Knee off Our Necks. Organizers called for Congress to pass policing reforms.

THE FUTURE OF BLM PROTESTS

Protests showed no sign of stopping in late 2020. For all the progress made, Black people are still more likely than white people to be killed by police officers. But there was hope. Activists held an event called the Commitment March in August in Washington, DC. The granddaughter of civil rights hero Dr. Martin Luther King Jr. spoke to the crowd. She said, "My generation has already taken to the streets, peacefully, and with masks, and socially distanced, to protest racism. We will fulfill the dream of my grandfather."[8]

GLOSSARY

activists

people who work to make social or political changes

anthem

a song of a specific group or nation

curfews

orders to ban people from traveling outside after a certain time

fascism

a system of government that is often racist, is led by a dictator, and tries to crush opposition

grand jury

a group of people who examine whether someone should be accused of a crime

hashtag

a word or words placed after the pound symbol (#) to identify specific topics in social media posts

pandemic

a disease outbreak in a large area or over the entire world

police brutality

the use of unnecessary force by officers against members of the public

SOURCE NOTES

INTRODUCTION: POLICE AND PROTESTERS

1. Quoted in Tom Gjelten, "Peaceful Protesters Tear-Gassed," *NPR News*, June 1, 2020. www.npr.org.

CHAPTER ONE: WHY HAVE BLM PROTESTS HAPPENED?

2. Quoted in "Michael Brown's Dad Appeals for Calm in Ferguson," *NBC News*, November 20, 2014. www.nbcnews.com.

CHAPTER THREE: WHAT WERE THE RESPONSES TO THE PROTESTS?

3. Quoted in Lois Beckett, "Nearly All Black Lives Matter Protests Are Peaceful Despite Trump Narrative, Report Finds," *Guardian*, September 5, 2020. www.theguardian.com.

4. Quoted in Chris McGreal, "Federal Agents Show Stronger Force at Portland Protests Despite Order to Withdraw," *Guardian*, July 20, 2020. www.theguardian.com.

CHAPTER FOUR: WHAT HAVE BLM PROTESTS ACCOMPLISHED?

5. Quoted in Elaine Godfrey, "The Enormous Scale of This Movement," *Atlantic*, June 7, 2020. www.theatlantic.com.

6. Quoted in Darcy Costello, et al., "Kentucky Grand Jury Indicts 1 of 3 Police Officers in Fatal Breonna Taylor Shooting," *USA Today*, September 24, 2020. www.usatoday.com.

7. Quoted in Eliott C. McLaughlin, "Honoring the Unforgivable," *CNN*, June 17, 2020. www.cnn.com.

8. Quoted in Sophia Barnes, "Commitment March on Washington 2020," *Channel 4 Washington*, August 28, 2020. www.nbcwashington.com.

FOR FURTHER RESEARCH

BOOKS

Samantha S. Bell, *The Rise of the Black Lives Matter Movement*. San Diego, CA: BrightPoint, 2021.

B. A. Hoena and Sam Ledoyen, *Colin Kaepernick*. Minneapolis, MN: Graphic Universe, 2020.

Wade Hudson and Cheryl Willis Hudson, eds., *We Rise, We Resist, We Raise Our Voices*. New York: Crown Books for Young Readers, 2018.

Philip Wolny, *The Police and Excessive Use of Force*. San Diego, CA: BrightPoint, 2021.

INTERNET SOURCES

Megan Gray, "Teenagers Lead the Way in Black Lives Matter Movement," *Portland Press Herald*, July 12, 2020. www.pressherald.com.

Derrick Bryson Taylor, "George Floyd Protests: A Timeline," *New York Times*, July 10, 2020. www.nytimes.com.

"Teens Talk About Encounters with Injustice and Police Violence," *PBS News Hour*, June 9, 2020. www.pbs.org.

WEBSITES

Black Lives Matter
www.blacklivesmatter.com

The official Black Lives Matter website gives updates on BLM's actions throughout the country. It also shares the history of BLM.

The National Association for the Advancement of Colored People (NAACP)
www.naacp.org

The NAACP is the largest organization in the United States dedicated to civil rights. The organization works toward equal rights for all in politics, education, society, and the economy. Its ultimate goal is to end race-based discrimination and improve the lives of all people.

National Museum of African American History and Culture
https://nmaahc.si.edu

The National Museum of African American History and Culture features information about Black history, including the protest movements of the past and present.

INDEX

IMAGE CREDITS

ABOUT THE AUTHOR

Clara MacCarald is a freelance writer with a master's degree in biology. She lives with her family in an off-grid house nestled in the forests of central New York. When not parenting her daughter, she spends her time writing nonfiction books for kids.